Where There Is No Freedom or Peace, There Is No Life

To JOHN
Love Erica

Erica Friday

WHERE THERE IS NO FREEDOM OR PEACE THERE IS NO LIFE

Published by Elite Publishing Academy, Allia Business Centre, Kings Hedges Road, Cambridge, CB4 2HY, United Kingdom

www.ElitePublishingAcademy.com

Cover Design: www.ElitePublishingAcademy.com

First printed 2022. Printed in the United Kingdom, www.ElitePublishingAcademy.com

ISBN Paperback - 978-1-912713-47-9
ISBN eBook - 978-1-912713-48-6

Where There Is No Freedom or Peace There Is No Life

When there is no freedom and happiness, there is no life.

There are people who suffered abuse, insult, isolation and humiliation, and they never experienced happiness and freedom from their childhood, into adulthood, and in some cases until they become older age I believe this is especially true of African women.

I am one of the women who has once never experienced happiness and freedom in life, but has suffered abuse, insult and humiliation. When there is no freedom and happiness there is no life.

I was born in Salisbury (1964) which was then the capital of Rhodesia. Now it is called Harare and is the capital of Zimbabwe. I was the first of a family of nine children of the same mother and the same father. We are five girls and four boys.

I grew up in the district of Bindura and started going to school at the age of seven in January 1971. I schooled there walking five miles to school and five miles back, Monday to Friday. On Saturdays and Sundays, I helped my mother to fields and do house chore. In school holidays my siblings used to visit our father in the city for two weeks with my mother. My father was working as a bus driver in the city of Salisbury which is called Harare now.

Due to the nature of my father's job, as a bus driver he would only come to visit once a year on Christmas holidays only.

So during school holidays, my siblings used to visit our father, while I stay behind with my grandmother, taking care of livestock and crops. It was a difficult time for me as the responsibilities were may far too much for my age.

I couldn't go further with education, so in December 1977 after completing my grade 7: I dropped school because my father couldn't afford to pay the school fees for my secondary education, as he earned so little.

When I dropped school, I joined my mothering her daily activities on the fields, which included land tilling, taking care of livestock's as well as routine house chore, again my siblings were still young, so I had to take care all of them as well.

My father was a bread winner even though, his desire was for all his children to learn how to read and write.

His desires could not be achieved due to limited income.

My father had built a round thatched hut, which we used as a kitchen. There was a three bedroomed house built of mud and poles. Another round thatched hut was a storeroom for crops after harvest. My mother kept a flock ten sheep, fifteen goats, lots of chickens and a herd of ten cows.

In 1978 after dropping school, I would wake up daily in the mornings, did all the housework, prepared food for the other children and went to the farm. Our field was two miles from the village and I had to leave home every morning around seven o'clock to work there. I didn't get home until six in the evening each day, except Sundays. On my way home, I fetched water and firewood for the house. On Sundays we would usually attend church as a family

One day in 1978 at dusk, It was end of August and I had just turned fourteen years, I was on my way from the field I stopped by a stream to wash off all the dust from the field and to fetch water to take home. After I finished washing and filled my bucket with water, I was just about to leave, when I heard a rustling noise behind me. I looked round and saw a man wearing camouflage. He carried a gun and was festooned with bullets. His eyes were red and he looked as if he had not slept for days.

I thought I was dreaming and I wiped my face with my hand. I looked again but saw the same person. I dropped the bucket because I was so frightened and started shivering.

"Hello, young girl, I am a Comrade. I am not going to hurt you," he said the man.

I realised that he was one of the people I had been warned about by the Rhodesian soldiers. They had told us that the comrades were terrorists who would kill us. I knelt down and started to beg him, "Please, don't kill me. I am coming from the farm and I stopped at this stream to fetch water. Please, please, don't kill me," I mumbled.

"Stand up and tell me your name," the comrade ordered.

I stood up, shivering with tears running down my face.

"My name is Eva and I live in that village with my mother," I murmured, pointing to the East with one finger.

"You're such a beautiful girl. I want you to go home now as it's becoming dark and when you get home, tell your mother that you met a comrade. Don't tell anyone besides your mother," the comrade said.

He picked up the bucket, which I had dropped, filled it with water and helped me to carry it. I was still not comfortable, as I was shivering and scared. I thanked him and left for home. My heart was racing but I didn't look back until I got home. I had not realised that the comrade had followed me home.

When I got home my mother had finished preparing food, but she was worried because I was a bit late. I entered the kitchen straight away without knocking. I was shivering, looking terribly distressed. My mother and the other children looked astounded.

"Oh, I was worried. Where have you been, Eva, and what happened to you?" my mother asked.

I couldn't answer. I was still shaking and suddenly I burst into floods of tears.

"Tell me what has happened," mother asked again.

I couldn't answer. I was now sobbing silently as I looked at my mother.

"I said what happened? Tell me now!" mother repeated angrily.

"Don't be angry with your daughter. It is all my fault," the comrade told her.

Everybody in the house looked at the doorway, where the voice was coming from, and saw the man. When mother set eyes on a man carrying a gun and draped in bullets, she couldn't say a word, she was so afraid and terrified. The other children hid themselves behind our mother. I didn't move from where I was standing, but I was even more scared as I thought that the comrade had followed me to kill me and my family.

Everyone went quite, no movements, no sound of anything, it was a moment of silent in the house, because it was scary to say anything. After about ten seconds the man covered with bullets and carrying a gun introduced himself to my mother.

"I am not a bad person and didn't come to hurt anyone, but to liberate this country and you people from the white minority regime. What I want is for your children to go and call all the people of this village now. We want food," the comrade said.

"Okay, I will do as you say," my mother said curtly. She ordered me, one of my sisters and two of my brothers to go to every house in the village and to tell everyone to come and meet a special visitor. Mother warned us not mention the word 'comrade' to people because they had heard on the radio news that comrades were bad and were cruel killers.

I left with the other three children to summon the villagers, I was anxious, as I thought that by the time we came back my mother and the other children would be dead.

Within short time and it was becoming dark, people were gathered outside my parents' home in a village of some fifty people: some married, some single, some widows and some young children. People kept quiet, scared, and disturbed, some were shivering, they were all terrified. The man introduced himself to the villagers. All people were ordered to sit down by the comrade.

"I am a comrade. My name is Freedom. I am not a bad person, as you hear on the news. I want to free you people and myself from being colonised by white people. I want to liberate this country," the comrade rasped.

"I am not alone. We are many and we want you people to make food for us. We eat meat, chickens but we don't eat vegetables," he said gruffly

After the comrade instructed what he wanted cooked, people stood up and told each other what to do. Some slaughtered chickens, some made a fire in another round thatched hut and started cooking 'sadza', our traditional corn porridge, and some women started cooking chickens in another kitchen, and the teenage girls were kept busy helping the women. Everybody was busy doing something. Lads went to patrol around the whole village to make sure that the Rhodesian army was not near. I was still uneasy. My heart was beating wildly and I was asking myself what was going to happen if Rhodesian soldiers did come across these comrades.

The comrade was walking up and down, looking at all the activities, until finally people had finished the cooking.

"The food is ready," mother informed the comrade.

"Bring all the food outside the houses," the comrade ordered.

Men and women helped each other to bring the food, and then very quickly the yard was full of comrades – approximately twenty and no-one saw where the other comrades came from as it was dark. We couldn't count them exactly because they didn't stay still but wandered about. It was also too scary to examine them closely for long.

The comrades served themselves the food and ate the food as they stood around – then they vanished, though no one saw where they went and which direction they took' People collected all plates and pots they used to make food and hid them in one of the rooms, then soon went back to their houses. Everybody was scared that Rhodesian soldiers might come and find them. If the villagers were found gathered together, they would be suspected and so would be in trouble.

Six days later another group of comrades came to our village again and ordered people to slaughter goats and cook for them. It was at the sunset and they went into the bush and hid on the mountain side near our village.

People finished slaughtering the goats and gave the meat to the women to cook with other traditional food. Then lads and young girls, including myself, took the food into the bush on the mountainside and gave it to the comrades. While they were eating, the lads were patrolling, looking to see if there were any soldiers about. We young girls sat with the comrades, talking to them and making them feel safe.

Feeding the comrades like this went on for about a month till end of September and the Rhodesian soldiers heard rumours that comrades had visited our village and other neighbouring villages and were being fed by us. The Rhodesian soldiers were the minority regime and the comrades were their enemies.

One morning a group of comrades had ordered food from a neighbouring village which was one mile from our village. People in our village were not aware that the comrades were hiding in the bush near the mountain and had ordered the food from our neighbouring village.

Soldiers had a tip-off of what was happening that morning, soldiers hided themselves so they could watch through binoculars all that had happened in that bush near the mountainside as people carried buckets of food and baskets of bread to go and feed the comrades.

That morning I woke up and prepared myself to go to the field as usual. It was one of those sunny, lazy mornings around 6am and it was Tuesday the second of October 1978. I left home and started jogging down the road towards the farm with a bucket in my hand, when suddenly I heard the noise of shooting all around.

I knew something seriously was happening, but I didn't know what to do. I supposed that the soldiers and comrades had clashed or came across each other.

I dropped down at the side of the road and lay on my stomach. I didn't know that the soldiers were in ambush all around me. The soldiers had already seen me but I didn't see them.

One of them whispered to me informing me to stay still and this is when I have noticed that I was surrounded with soldiers.

When I realised I was in the middle of the battle between the soldiers and comrades, I crawled behind a tree and into some long grass to hide myself. One of the soldiers crawled towards me and ordered me to stay where I was lying on my stomach and keep my head down, It was a serious and scary situation, as the shootings went on for about twenty minutes.

People of my village were hurt and some killed, and many others in neighbouring village. Livestock, crops and houses were destroyed, as soldiers set fire to the houses. There were army trucks and soldiers everywhere and didn't know where they were coming from.

I survived that battle, though I had been absolutely petrified. It was like a nightmare. All wounded people and other survivors, including myself, were bundled into army trucks, where there were white soldiers, painted themselves with black charcoal and two black soldiers. We set off in convoy for the nearest Rhodesian temporary Army Camp which was near the growth point. The camp was built with tents not with bricks.

One of the black soldiers shouted at everyone in the truck that we were going to be grilled and, if we didn't tell the truth, he was going to deal with everyone who was in the army trucks once and for all. He shouted at us that we should tell all we knew about the comrades and where I was taking the bucket.

On the way we passed through our village and some neighbouring villages, where we could see many people lying on the ground. It was awful and devastated

When I saw people lying on the ground scattered everywhere, I was confused with fear because I didn't know if they were all dead., I looked, wondering if I would recognise anyone but didn't because the truck was moving. I didn't see any of my family in the truck, I assumed that they were among those people who were scattered everywhere. More villages were destroyed, The Rhodesian soldiers had won that battle because they had attacked from every both angles.

When we reached the army camp, I looked at every person who was there and tried to ask if anyone had seen my mother or one of my family. No one seemed to want to talk to anyone. I spotted a man who lived near our home.

"Have you seen my mother?" I murmured. The man gave me a blank look and then shook his head. "I'm sorry," he said.

I didn't hear what else he said in the next five minutes because I couldn't hear anything. I just went blank, as I felt pins and needles running up and down my body. Then I doubled over and threw up over and over again. I felt someone put a coat round me. I turned and saw my mother, my cousin sister, and all my brothers.

Some of my cousins were caught in crossfire on their way to school and were shot but one of my cousin sisters and brothers were lucky to survive because they were still behind.

Everybody was crying for their beloved ones, because they didn't know whether their beloved ones had survived, or they were killed during the shootings.

"Oh, shut up, all of you! You were feeding terrorists," you are going to cry more than you're doing now. One of the soldiers barked, scowling at us.

People were called one by one from a big tent where everybody was seated. I was called to be questioned by one of the soldiers called Mike. He was a tall, slim, white officer. He had a thin moustache and was wearing a trilby hat. His rank was Major and he was in command of the camp and the soldiers, who used to call him 'Sir' or 'Chief'. I will never forget him because he brutally abused me.

"Have you ever seen comrades, girl?" Mike said accusingly.
"No, I never saw them," I murmured.

"Liar, you little girl! You were supposed to go to school, but you were carrying a bucket full of food. Where were you going, you stupid girl? Take her away. I want to teach her a lesson," she is going to tell me all what she knows after dealing with her "Mike" said angrily.

He blew out a cloud of smoke from the cigarette he was puffing - he smoked like a chimney. I was shivering and the hairs pricked the back of my neck. Mike stuffed his hands in his pockets and began to walk up and down the room.

I was taken to another room with one of the soldiers, and Mike followed me. He told me to kneel down on the floor beside a bucket of water. My head was covered with a black cloth and Mike ordered another soldier to push my head into the bucket full of water. After some seconds he pulled my head out again. He then began to beat me with a stick and kept on beating.

After that Mike ordered the other soldier to leave the room. Mike then forced himself in me, destroying my virginity. I bled a lot and was in severe pain. He warned me not to tell anyone, because if I could tell anyone he would kill me and my family.

When Mike saw that I was so distraught, he ordered me to go and join the other people who had been questioned. As I went out of that room to the tent, I couldn't walk properly because I was in such pain. I didn't tell anyone, even my mother, what had happened to me. Every part of my body was in pain and I was tired and terrified.

My mother was in the tent with other people. She had noticed that I was not myself, but she hadn't known what was happening to me. We all slept in the same tent that night. The next morning, we were divided into two groups, men in one tent and women in another.

People were beaten, interrogated about the comrade's whereabouts, but apparently no one told the soldiers the truth, because the villagers feared the comrades.
I was even more scared of the comrades, thinking that if I told the soldiers about them, I would lose the rest of my family. The comrades had warned villagers not to say anything to anyone, especially not to the soldiers. They said that, whatever situation we were in, they would kill each and every family if anyone betrayed them.

Villagers had already lost some of their relatives and lost their homes, so they didn't want any more problems. The soldiers kept interrogating people day after day.

On the third day I was taken to another room, and I was sexually abused again with the same soldier. I really suffered physically and mentally and it was awful.

My mother was beaten all the time she has been interrogated, seeing my mother's face swollen, her eyes became red was particularly awful for me. I was terrified, confused. I crawled to where my mother was

16

seated after being beaten by soldiers and whispered to her ear.

"Mother, I am going to tell the soldiers all I know about the comrades. If I don't, they will keep on hurting us.

"No, don't make things worse. I have lost some of my family and I don't want to lose you as well," mother begged.

I heeded what my mother had said and kept quiet. People were herded at the camp for six weeks and after six weeks all the older people and their surviving families including my mother were released to go back to their villages. They were provided with food such as tinned food and tents for temporary accommodation until they had rebuilt their homes. All the dead villagers, including my cousin sisters and cousin brothers, were buried in different places with other people who survived and managed to escaped from being bundled in the trucks and taken to the camp.

I remained behind in the camp with other young people and I was the youngest girl in the group. Soldiers would rape young women who were left behind the camp whenever they feel like. It was particularly awful for me as I was so young (fourteen years) and in so much confused.

I got used to the routine of being in the sexual abused, as I had no choice because was scared of my life. I recovered from the beatings slowly and gradually healed. I was always quiet, thinking about what was going to happen in my life, what my future would be like, but I could find no answers.

The soldiers started to trust me, and I was chosen to be a leader of the group of women who were left behind. I was given the gate keys as the camp was fenced and there was a gate. The soldiers were sending me on errands with other young women to buy them cigarettes at the nearest shops. They allowed me to go for a walk once a week with some other women, but we were not allowed to go more than five hundred metres from the camp. I was not allowed to talk to any man outside or even inside the camp. Every evening at 4pm we were all locked in.

Gerald, one of the village men, had been chosen to cook food for the soldiers and do Mike's laundry.

Mike ordered that I should go to his room once a week to clean it. He used to rape me when I went to his room every week. Sometimes he would send the cook to call me in the middle of the night when I was sleeping. I couldn't resist but had to obey every order and sometimes he came by himself to harassed me, telling me to go and lock the gate, and this was a way of telling me to go to his room and forced himself in me. Day and night soldiers guarded the whole camp.

One day I sat down and folded my arms, it was in the beginning of December 1978. I thought about killing myself because of all my suffering. Others of my age were at school but I had not been able to continue my education. If only my father had had the money to keep me in school, I might not have suffered all these misfortunes.

That night I was in awful pain and was so depressed and angry at being brutally raped. Also seeing other women suffer that I thought of escape. But how could I, that was the big question. So, as I couldn't sleep, I lay there listening to what the soldiers were saying.

"Around mid-midnight, 'Mike called loudly to all the soldiers around the camp.

I have received a radio report that terrorists are operating at Darwin village. We have to go and fight them before they attack us," Mike said angrily and he ordered the lower ranks to start preparing for the journey the first thing tomorrow.

"We should leave camp tomorrow in the evening," he said.

"OK, sir. Everything will be ready by noon tomorrow," said the sergeant humbly.

Darwin village was about two hundred to three hundred kilometres from the camp. Mike had decided that troop 2 would go on the mission and troop 1 would stay behind in camp.

When I woke up the next day, I saw that all the soldiers were busy packing equipment and belongings in their trucks.

"Can you come and unlock the food store now?" Gerald the cook asked me curtly.

I went and unlocked the room and Gerald asked me to help him in the kitchen for the first time. I refused, saying that I was scared of Mike as he didn't like to see me near other men. The cook told me not to worry.

While I was helping him in the kitchen, he told me about the departure of a troop to Darwin village and advised me to escape while they were leaving.

"No, I can't escape. If they catch me, what will happen? They will kill me straight away. No, I can't do it!" I said anxiously.

"Yes, you can, and I am going to help you. I am worried about you. You're like my daughter and you're so young. What is happening to you pains me a lot. I want you to leave this place, even if it means I get killed because of you. I'd rather die than see you being abused before my eyes. No, I will help you. Just keep your mouth shut and follow all that I tell you to do. Okay?" the cook explained fervently.

I was scared of agreeing to what the cook had suggested to me, but because I had always been a very confident young girl, I wanted to try it. Escaping was in my mind all along, but how to do it was the real issue.

It started pouring with rain in the afternoon, while the soldiers were still packing their belongings in the trucks. The soldiers finished packing and went inside the tents to wait to start their journey.

Major Mike told the cook that he wanted to see me before he left for battle. I went to Mike's room as usual and he forced himself in me. He didn't care how much I was in pain, he just wanted to take his pleasure. I asked Mike if I could go and rest in the food store because I was tired and not feeling well. He allowed me to do that but warned me to be a good girl while he was away.

The cook came to the food store and saw me sitting sobbing silently

"What happened? Why are you crying?" he asked.

"He did it again and I am in pain," I answered.

"Be brave now, I heard them talking about leaving in thirty minutes, and they asked me to load all these boxes of food into that Land Rover, and cover the food with tents. So, I will tell you what to do. I want you to be confident," the cook quietly explained.

"Okay, I will do as you said," I murmured.

He loaded up the boxes of food and covered them with tents. When he finished it was still pouring, with some rolls of thunder. The sky was dark with storm clouds. It was still afternoon, but it felt like evening.

At about 3p.m. the soldiers were ready to go and they shouted to each other, saying, "Hurry up, it's time to go and deal with the terrorists."

Gerald told me to get into the Land Rover which he had loaded with food. He covered me with a tent, leaving a small gap for me to breathe. No one noticed me hidden in the back of the car.

The major and his troop got in their trucks and started the journey. It took them three hours to reach their destination. They passed villages, shops and busy road junctions, where stallholders and street hawkers competed noisily for trade.

It was evening-time around 6pm, when the soldiers reached Darwin village. They stopped and parked their vehicles near the shops. People from nearby came out of their houses and started gazing at the army vehicles. Some soldiers got out of them and began smoking. Other soldiers walked up and down looking suspiciously at everything. When the villagers saw the fleet of army vehicles, they knew that something was wrong. It was rare to see soldiers camping in the bush or visiting shops. I could see everything that was happening through a small gap, but I was too scared to move.

Soldiers started talking to people, trying to be friendly, because they knew people didn't like nor trust them. As I carefully crept out of the truck, I made a low noise, which the soldiers heard. Fortunately, there was a dog passing by so the soldiers assumed that it was the dog which had made the noise. I looked up and down the road and either sides of the truck but saw no one, so I set off without being seen, slowly walking to the nearby village.

When I reached it, I stepped into the first yard and dogs started barking at me. I tried to stop them by saying 'shi-shi' but they continued barking loudly. The owner of the dogs came outside and shouted to ask who was there.

"Please help me," I whispered.

The man took me inside the house and asked who I was and where I had come from. I asked him to hide me and I promised to tell him everything later. The man's name was Jacob and he was married with two children, one son and a daughter.

Within minutes we heard more barking and footsteps outside. Jacob quickly hid me behind the door where there were two sacks full of maize. He went outside to check on his dogs and he found the yard full of soldiers. They wanted to know why the dogs were barking, but Jacob told them that his son had just come from putting the cows into the kraal. The soldiers demanded to see the boy, so he was shown to them. One soldier entered the house and I could hear the soldier's foot step entering the house while I was hidden behind the door. After they talked and talked to Jacob, telling him that, if there was a problem or if he needed help, he should come to get them. The soldiers had also told Jacob that he should tell the people of the nearby villages that they were going to be at their campsite for some time and, if any villagers heard of the whereabouts of the enemy, they should inform the soldiers. The soldiers then left the house and went back to their cars.

Jacob made sure that the soldiers had gone and there was no one outside or near the house except his dogs. Then he came inside and ordered me to come out from the hiding place and give him an explanation.

I explained the whole story and didn't want him to feel pity for me. I asked him if he could find me somewhere to hide me. He agreed to take me to another village which was about fifteen miles away.

Jacob told no one except his wife that he was going to another village that night

We started the journey at midnight. The weather was very bad, pouring down with rain. We reached the other village after 4am. We couldn't walk fast because I was exhausted and had pains everywhere and Jacob carried me on his bicycle.

When we reached the village, it was already morning. Amos was a head of the village and he and his family lived in the village of ten houses. Amos was married to two wives and has nine children, some were grown up and some were still young. Amos was a kind man, understanding, and talkative. Amos and Jacob has been friends for many years and trusted each other

Jacob went into a house, leaving me sitting outside. He asked Amos to allow me to stay with him and his family for a while, after telling him my terrible story.

Jacob left me in the hands of Amos and went back that early morning. to his own village. I stayed at the village for about four weeks. All the time I was indoors and came outside early morning and at night to use the toilet accompanied by the Amos's wife or one of his children. It was stressful and I was terrified, but I had no choice. Christmas time came, other children were happy outside singing, running around, throwing balls but I was inside a small house which used to keep harvest crops. I couldn't join other children because of my condition.

The second week of January 1979, Amos asked me if I knew where my father was working. I didn't know but I knew the name of the bus company he drove for. The Third week same month in January, Amos went to the city to find out if he could locate my father at the bus company I had named. He warned me not to let myself be seen, but to stay indoors until he came back. He promised me that, if he found my father, he would take me to him. When he got to the city, he chased around looking for my father, only to find out that he had been arrested three days after the battle between Rhodesians soldiers and comrades which happened in our village. He was utterly stunned and so he came back home next day.

"I am sorry, Eva. Your father was arrested three days after the battle which happened at your village" Amos stammered. When my father heard that, there was a battle at our village, he drove to the village after three days thinking he would found his family and take them to the city, but he was unfortune and met the soldiers along the way. My father was arrested and was sent to prison for three years. This is how my father was arrested in October 1978

I was confused, distressed, and kept quiet for some time thinking what was going to happen to me if these soldiers find me. I then started sobbing silently until my stomach hurts. I had thought my problems would be over if my father was found, but with my father arrested, what should I do? The soldiers would find me one day. I could not go back to my own village because I was on the death list of both the comrades and the soldiers. I talked to myself silently, trying to find a way out of my impossible situation

I stayed another week, thinking of the next to do with my situation, in the house alone. I couldn't eat. I was completely terrified and even more depressed.

One evening that same week I went outside by myself to go to the toilet, when the dogs started barking till Amos quietened them. I thought at first that the dogs had been barking at me, as it was the first time I had gone outside by myself. In all the previous weeks staying there. The dogs, however, were barking at some comrades who had come to the village that night to order the villagers to cook food for them. This was the first time; the comrades have visited them. This was no surprise to me, as I had seen the comrades before. Seeing them again, I reflected on what had happened at my village when the comrades and soldiers had fought. I was afraid that it could happen again.

The villagers cooked and served the food to the comrades. After eating, the comrades and villagers started to sing liberation songs and continued until midnight. I had joined the crowd of villagers and comrades, but no one noticed that I was a stranger because it was night. Some villagers may have thought that I had come with the comrades. After midnight the comrades disappeared, though no one saw how they left the village.

The comrades were scared that, if they told the villagers their plans, they would be betrayed to the soldiers, who used to come with tinned food or other supplies to give to the villagers to encourage them to give information about the comrades.

After a week around 4am in February 1979, a man came from another village to order all the people of Amos's village to prepare food for the comrades before sunrise. While the villagers were running up and down getting the food ready, they didn't know that soldiers had been tipped off about what was happening. I assumed that someone from the same village had tipped the soldiers about the comrades' visits. That time Amos was allowing me to mingle with some of his children in the house of his first wife.

The soldiers laid in the hiding bush, letting the villagers finish cooking the food and waiting for them to go to deliver it to the comrades. When the food was cooked, men, women, and teenage girls and boys took it to the base where the comrades were hidden. I joined them, carrying two baskets of bread and this was before sunrise.

The soldiers waited for the whole day watching all the movements. The lads were patrolling up and down the whole day checking if there were soldiers nearby. The comrades were hidden at the mountain side in the bush the whole day. Comrades used travel from village to village during nights and spent the days sleeping in the bush.

The day passed and it was evening around 6pm, and people were now trying to go back to their villages carryings empty baskets, buckets. The soldiers started firing at the base and at everyone who was around the comrades. A helicopter appeared overhead.

What was happening was exactly like what had happened at my village. People were being shot by soldiers. Comrades were returning fire to the soldiers, but they had no chance because the soldiers had greater firepower, It was terrifying.

As all this was happening, I and some of the villagers were running towards a river. I didn't know where I was going or what I was going to do as it was becoming dark so, I just followed the others.

I thought that I was a dead person, that I could not possibly survive a second battle. As I ran I heard a sharp noise and saw a bright light flash before my eyes. That was that. Everything went blank!

In March I found myself in hospital with a lot of bandages on my head, body, legs and arms. I didn't know what had happened as I had lost my memory.

All I could remember was pain and I could not get up by myself from hospital bed for three months. Nurses washed me and changed the hospital gown while I lay in bed, I couldn't eat by myself but fed by tubes.

I started to regain my memory after six months in September 1979, I was in a ward with other people who had been injured in the war. They were from all over Zimbabwe and some had lost their legs, some their arms.

One day I asked a nurse how I came to be in the hospital, and what had happened to me.

"When you were admitted to this hospital, you were unconscious and terrible injured." the nurse said.

"Who brought me to the hospital and what happened to my head?" I asked, with tears running down my cheeks

"You need to rest now," the nurse sighed. She gave me an injection to calm me and I slept. The next day a group of doctors came and surrounded my bed. They closed the curtains and started to examine my head.

I asked them what the problem was with my head. One of the doctors asked my name, and I told him. They looked at each other and smiled.

"Do you remember what happened to you, Eva?" a doctor asked.

"No, I don't know what happened, but I remember hearing a sharp noise and seeing fire in my eyes," I stammered.

"Ok, can you remember other things?" the doctor asked.

"No, I cannot remember tell me what happened to me, please," I pleaded

"You" were injured in the head fortunately, the most important part of the head was not injured, but you were very badly hurt. You were brought in by some soldiers. They found you on the sand near the river among other injured people," the doctor explained carefully.

"Oh, it's now coming in my mind, I can remember that there was a battle, soldiers were firing guns at villagers and comrades, and I was among the villagers remembering running towards the river it was terrifying I mumbled. I could not say much but started, as all the bad memories of the first battle came back to me. I was now weeping until the doctor instructed the nurse to give me something to calm me down and then I slept.

Weeks and months passed, and my wounds were healing slowly. I could sit up and even walk on crutches just for a few steps. I could remember most of the events which had happened in my past.

On the 12 December 1979 around 6pm. I was sitting on the hospital bed looking at the window, waiting for my evening medication and I could see people Outside singing liberation songs and dancing. I was confused, because they were dancing like comrades.

"We are independent!" a nurse shouted, entering our ward. "The war is over. People are going to be reunited with their relatives," the nurse shouted cheerly entering our ward.

Every patient who had the strength shouted for independence. The ward throbbed with noise.

I looked straight to the nurse and asked her to tell me what had happened. She sat down near my bed and explained everything to all the patients. There was both sadness and happiness because most people had lost relatives during the war. I was particularly upset because I had lost cousin sisters, brothers, and I didn't know whether my mother and my other siblings were still alive. I was injured and I didn't know where to go from the hospital. I was confused and felt that my life was empty and I was very depressed by the thought that I had no future.)

"Why are you so quiet? You should be happy that the war is over, cheer up!" one of the other patients said.

"I don't know if I have anyone who survived. All my people seemed were killed and I don't know what I'll do after I leave hospital.

"Oh, sorry I didn't know," she apologised.

When I had escaped from the army camp, the troop of soldiers who was left behind had discovered that I was not among other young women in the Army camp. Some of the soldiers had gone to my village and harassed my family, because they thought that, having escaped I had gone back home to hide. When my family was interrogated and harassed by the soldiers, my mother began to think that the soldiers had killed me. No-one didn't know that I escaped with the other troop to Darwin and I was in hospital.

When the war was over, my mother heard rumours that I had been killed in the battle at Darwin. She didn't know that I had survived, seriously injured. She travelled to Darwin and visited the district hospital of Darwin and searched, hoping she would be able to find the truth of course, she had no success.

According to the nurses, I was brought to the Central Hospital which is now called Harare hospital by soldiers who found me and others on the river sand near the river while we were unconscious.

My most severe injury was my head wound, and the nurses dressed it every day with lots of bandages. I had been very lucky, as I could have died. I couldn't remember the name of our village or my mother's name. I used to lose my memory and then regain it.

Whenever my memory came back, I would think of my future and what happened then started sobbing silently. I wouldn't be able to sleep and would suffer severe pain. There was a woman in a nearby bed who kept asking me questions – the sort of questions you don't ask people when they are in distress.

My mother had no hope of seeing me again, and I didn't have any hope of seeing my family again. I remember very much it was Sunday the 22nd of December 1979. I asked the nurse to take me outside so that I could feel the sun. It was the first time I'd been outside the ward since I had been admitted to the hospital.

"Good afternoon, nurse," a woman said gently

"Good afternoon. What can I do for you?" a nurse asked.

"I am looking for a girl named Eva. I understand she is in this hospital, and I was directed to you by people in that ward," the woman answered, pointing at my ward.

"Oh, sit down, madam. Who are you to this girl, Eva?" the nurse asked.

"She is my daughter and I have been looking everywhere. I thought she had been killed during the war, but I couldn't rest until I had checked every hospital. When I got to reception here, I was directed to Ward C and people in the ward directed me to you. Do you have any information please?" the woman begged, she hadn't recognised me and I hadn't recognised her too but I had heard what she said.

This woman was my mother but didn't recognise her. She was tall and very beautiful, light in complexion, always smiling and very polite.

This was her last hope because it the biggest one in the capital city of Rhodesia which is now called Harare. It was called Central Hospitalor ku Gomo which is now called Harare Hospital. This is where most black people were admitted and treated especially those who were injured in war and had complications.

It was a very good hospital with good qualities and well maintained.

Most doctors were white and few black doctors and they were also few black nurses and more white nurses. All patients were being looked after well with respect and dignity.

"OK, let's go back in the ward, it's becoming cold. "the nurse said"

I was sitting on the wheel chair and the nurse started pushing it going back to the ward. Mother was behind following us to the ward.

When we got back to the ward, the nurse sat me on the bed. She then asked the woman to follow her to the office where the Matron was. The matron was a white woman, tall, slim and cheerful. I never knew her name as the nurses and doctors were calling her Matron all the time, as for us patients we used to speak with the nurses on duty if you need anything. The Matron was on her mid 40s of age, full of energy always making herself busy when she was on duty. They were young, older, black, white nurses and doctors working at this hospital,

Nurse knocked the door of the office and Matron asked the nurse to come in. The nurse told the woman to wait outside of the office till she comes back to fetch her. Within minutes nurse came out of the office and asked the woman to follow in the office.

They spent almost thirty minutes in the office, and I could hear them talking but didn't know what exactly they were discussing. I assumed that they were speaking about the person the woman (my mother) was looking for.

The Matron had asked the woman (mother) some security question and she had answered most of them correctly, and also identified the birth mark which was on one of my breast. She also carried the pictures and my birth certificate where ever she was going looking for me. Matron and the nurse seeing that information they all believed that she was telling the true.

The matron, came out and left the nurse and woman (mother) in her office. The matron walked towards my hospital bed. She grabbed a chair and sat down then started talking to me in a nice way. She was just talking about my health, that I was doing well and recovering well.

She then explained to me about why the woman (mother) in the office had visited the hospital. The matron narrated all what she had asked a woman (mother) whom she had left in her office with the nurse. The matron believed that the woman was my mother so she wanted me to meet her, if I was happy to do that.

Eva, can you remember anything about your mother, how she looks like and how beautiful she is? Matron smiled.

I smiled back to her and said I don't know maybe if I see her I can remember. The matron said is there anything you which you can identify about the woman (mother) who is in the office with nurse Monalisa.

Who is nurse Monalisa 'I asked' because I never knew the name of nurse though it was written on the badge which she used to wear with her uniform. I used to call her nurse all the time she was looking after me.

When she asked; if I can identify anything about the woman (mother) whom she left behind in her office with nurse Monalisa, I answered her that I don't know if I can remember her:

I was not comfortable talking to the matron as I never saw her talking to any patient in the ward. She was always in her office talking on the phone and she used to be seen coming in hospital and straight to her office and going out of hospital after work.

The matron was a well-respected woman despite her job title but because of her race which was white.

Eva I think I have good news for you, the woman in my office might be your mother.

I paused for about two second then I said to the Matron, how do you know is my mother and why is she in your office?

I wanted to speak with you first, before I bring her to you, because I didn't know how you were going to take it. 'The matron explained'

How do you feel about what I have just told you? 'The matron asked'

I don't know how I am feeling but I want to see her and touch her hand. I replied the matron.

Alright, I am going to tell the woman (mother) to come and meet you, the matron informed me politely.

''Excuse me' 'I will be back in five minutes, the matron said.
She stood up from the chair she was sitting and walked to her office.
Within minutes the matron came back from the office and walked straight to my bed accompanied by the nurse Monalisa and the woman

Nurse Monalisa grabbed two chairs and added them to another chair which was already near my bed seated by the matron.

Madam, this is Eva: she is alive as we have explained everything about how she was brought in this hospital and how injured she was. The Matron explained

The Matron and nurse Monalisa left for office and left the woman (mother) remaining sitting beside my bed.

I couldn't say anything as I was so emotional hearing that the woman sitting beside my bed was my mother but couldn't recognise my own mother.

This really frustrated me and I couldn't believe my own mother was alive and she has found me.

Eva my daughter, I have searched for you everywhere and I am so sorry that I didn't recognise you when I first saw you outside with the nurse. I am also very happy that I have found you. Mother explained

She moved her chair close to my bed and she wanted to hug me but she didn't know where to touch.

I was not the Eva she had known, my head was bandaged and was not looking good though I was in hospital for some months. I was recovering slowly, slowly and it was a long process for me to be normal again.

The food was saved and my mother asked nurse Monalisa, if she can feed me. This time I was being fed soft food with a special spoon. Nurse Monalisa explained to my mother that she could not feed me as they were complication and promised my mother that she will feed me when I am eating normal food. My mother looked disappointed and later understood why nurse Monalisa could not allow her to feed me. Observing how I was being fed made my mother to understand more, why the nurse didn't allow her to feed me

The nurse left after feeding me and she had also finished her shift for the day. She was returning on duty the following morning.

My mother asked to spend a night at hospital because it was too late for her to go back to the village and also wanted to spend more time with me.

The Matron allowed her to spend the night at hospital, she was quiet happy and held my hand, as I clutched hers and we spent the time quietly.

Mother was concerned about me, so I told her that I was much better than before. I explained what I could remember to her: how I had escaped and how I came to be in hospital. The nurses who were on night duty noticed that I was not asleep at about twelve midnight and one of the night nurses came and gave me tablets and I slept until the next morning.

According to my mother, she couldn't sleep, as she was checking on me all night

The next morning the doctors, nurse Monalis and the Matron arrived to do his rounds. Nurse Monalisa drew the curtain around my bed

"How are you feeling today, Eva?" one of the doctors asked.

"I am feeling better and I think I am fit enough to go home," I answered with a smile.

"Eva is very happy. Her mother is here and she is prepared to take Eva with her, if Eva is fit to go home," nurse Monalisa explained.

The doctor looked at me and we smiled at each other. Nurse Monalisa was very pleased that my mother had found me. After the round my mother was introduced to the doctors and she was greeted and welcomed. The doctor explained everything about my condition to my mother and the doctor asked my mother to be a bit patient as the doctor wanted to monitor my recovering for another week or so.

My mother listened and understood what the doctor has explained to her and she left for the village. Mother started visiting me once a week for about three weeks and I was doing very well, mentally and physically. My swelling legs were getting better and I could feel my body was getting better.

After three weeks, end of January 1980 I was discharged and given all the medication and bandages I would need.

I was told to come for check-ups at the hospital every month, and to go to the clinic for dressings once a week. I followed all these instructions from the doctors, and after four months I was making a good progress.

On the 18th April Zimbabwe gained official independence and people were very happy celebrating. I was happy that we gained independence but still hurting that most people including myself lost beloved ones and I nearly lost my life during liberation war. This haunted me every day.

In December 1980, I could walk on crutches and was trying to do things for myself. Mother was always there for me as I tried to forget about the past, but it was impossible and it was not easy to forget: people who were so close to me had died, so the pain would never go. It seemed as if it had happened yesterday. The people of Zimbabwe had got independence, but for me it seemed hollow]

On the 24th of December 1980 I visited our local shops, walking in a clutch as my right leg was still weak. It was not very far from my village and my mother used to send for some errands, to gain more exercises. When I got to the shops, I saw a tall, handsome, and dark in complexion, standing outside the shops leaning on the 404 blue car, which was parked in front of the shops, and he was drinking a pint of beer. People were happy playing music, dancing and doing some shopping for Christmas the following day. People of Zimbabwe felt independent and had freedom from the colonial regime.

This man saw me entering in the shop, he waved at me and I waved back. I bought a packet of sugar and a loaf of bread which my mother had asked me to go and buy.

I didn't spend more time in the shop, I got out the shop and started walking back home. The man followed me and started talking to me. He introduced himself as Peter and I also introduced myself to him.

We had a good chat and he asked for my number but I didn't have a phone, so I couldn't give him a phone number. He wrote his number inside of my palm and asked me to write it at a safe place when I get home. I told him that, there was no need for him to give me his number because there was nowhere to phone him

He confirmed that he had visited his aunt for Christmas holiday who lived at our neighbouring village so he promised to see me whenever he visits her again. He left me and returned back to the shops and I continued walking home.

I got home safely and told my mother about this man. Mother didn't say much but she asked me to be careful as she had become very protective. She didn't want to see me being hurt anyone again.

Peter started visiting his aunt more often, and after his aunt he visited me as our village which was not far from his aunt's. We continue seeing each other as friends for about a year, I started trusting Peter as a good friend and he was polite, good listener, and communicated very well. He was not judgemental person, so I started speaking with him freely but I never wanted to tell him about the sexual abuse I had experienced at my young age.

He also told me much about himself, he stated that he was an engineer and I believed him. He then stated that he was on holiday as he had just returned from Germany.

After dating for another year on the 29th of October 1984 we got married traditional. Immediately I moved to the city with him. Peter lived in Harare in the suburb called Hatfield and he was living alone before our marriage.

We stayed as couple happily for a year and I got pregnant in October 1985. Peter was posted to Romania at the beginning of February 1986, leaving me three-months pregnant. He was checking on me time to time through phoning and writing letters.

My mother used to come and check on me all the time. His friends were send by him to check on me time to time. His friends used to come in a flash and driving the arm trucks. This started to haunt me most of the times as I always reflected what had happened during the liberation war.

One day, I asked one of his friends how he became a soldier and explained to me that, they were trained together with Peter. He explained all in detail that Peter advanced in learning engineering, that why he was working as an engineer in Army. This is when it really started disturbing me. I hated soldiers with passion after being abused by soldier Mike.

I gave birth on the 9th of July 1986 to a healthy baby girl, she weighed eight pounds, very cute and light in complexion. Looked alike her mother.

Peter stayed in Romania for three years and came back to Zimbabwe in July 1989, so I brought up my baby girl with the help of my mother and other people who were around me.

When Peter returned from Romania our baby girl Lisa was three years old.

I got pregnant again in August 1989 and gave birth to a baby boy Tony in May 1990 and he weighed 5.5pounds, light in complexion. He looked alike me.

Peter got promoted to a rank of Major in December 1991 and he was working in Zimbabwe.

In 1992 in May he was posted to Congo left me with one month pregnant. Our girl Lisa was now five years and some months. Tony had just turned two years when Peter left for Congo

In 1993 I gave birth to a beautiful baby boy and he weighed 3.5kg. he looked very alike his father very dark in complexion

Peter stayed in Congo for two years and came back January 1994

Whatever love I may have had for Peter had long since died, as he had never been there when I most needed his love and support.

When he came back in October 1994, Peter was then promoted to the rank of colonel and commander of the

M'sasa Base, and became in charge of the Armoury base, which is the workshop for all the weapons and armoured cars of the Zimbabwe army.

Peter was now working in Zimbabwe without being posted out of the country. He was trying to do his best to make his family happy and provide for them.

The Zimbabwean government became tyrannical to its own people. Soldiers and police were corrupt, especially the higher ranks. Soldiers of the lower ranks were sent by high ranking officers to beat, torture innocent people. It was awful to see people suffering torture and being suffered by their own government because they had told the truth. When this had gone on for two years, I could no longer ignore it, so I joined the opposition party, which was formed in September 1999 by Tsvangirai and Sibanda. I started going to the meetings, though my husband was against it, as he didn't care about my feelings or the feelings of anyone else.

He was only concerned about himself, though I was not happy with anything as his wife. I thought of all that had happened to me during the war. I believed that, as Zimbabwean people had their independence, they should be enjoying their country, but they had started suffering more than before.

I thought day and night of how I could help the people of Zimbabwe, but who would listen to me. I tried to talk to my husband, as I knew that he had the opportunity to talk to his superiors and the minister of defence to stop the beating, torture of innocent people.

My husband didn't want to talk to his superiors because he was afraid that they would think that he was against the government. I became affected emotionally, particularly in my marriage. I asked myself so many times why I had got married to a soldier after all the difficult times I had gone through – I had nearly died because I had helped to liberate my country.

I was young but I had played a role in the war for independence what had I achieved in all that time, if our government now treated its own people so cruelly? I felt that my sacrifices and sufferings had been wasted, as I had wanted everyone to be treated fairly after liberation. Instead life for Zimbabweans was becoming more and more difficult.

In December 1999 my life was at stake once again. I didn't know that I was being followed everywhere I went. My husband had been warned by his superiors to stop me from giving support to the opposition party. He tried to persuade me to stop participating in the opposition party, but I wouldn't listen to him.

One Friday afternoon on the 10th of December 1999, about half past four, I was coming from my Peter's workplace with his driver. We stopped off at a shopping centre to pick up some groceries. While we were in the supermarket a man came and told the driver he should drop everything and leave the shop at once by another exit. He was advised not return to the car, but to take a taxi. The driver straightaway told me that we had to go, so we left.

I had left Peter in the office because he had told me that he wanted to clear his desk. He had been given a mission to take a group of ordinary soldiers to another town to beat up some people who had demonstrated about food prices.

I called Peter on the phone and told him what had happened. He advised me not to go to our house, but instead to go to his sister's.

"You can go to your house, and I will go my own way," I said to the driver.

"I cannot leave you on your own. It's not safe for you, ma'am," the driver protested

I told him not to worry and I instructed the taxi driver to drop us off, while I took another taxi to my husband's sister.

Peter left all he was doing and rushed home for the kids. Mr and Mrs White had collected our children and theirs from school. We used to give each other duties of taking children to school and collect them after school. So that day they had taken my children and their children to school and collected them from school.

They were very good people with children the same age as mine, and all the kids got on very well together. They had always been very supportive for me when my we moved near them.

When my husband got home, he collected the children and then called me to tell me that the kids were fine and safe. He insisted that I should leave for England the next day because my life was in danger. He told me that people thought I had been collecting information about the M'sasa Base workshop to give it to the opposition party.

"You should leave the country first thing tomorrow morning. I will arrange everything," my Peter said.

The next morning of Tuesday the 11th of December 1999, he instructed his driver to come and pick me from his sister's house and drove me to the airport. The driver brought me some money about three hundred pounds and a bag which contained my few clothes, which my husband had given to him to give me. I boarded a Ghanaian Airline plane that day around midday with tears running down my cheeks because I hadn't been able to say goodbye to my children. The plane went first to Ghana, where it stopped for two hours. It then continued its journey and we reached the UK next morning Wednesday of 12th of December 1999 at 6 o'clock. am

At Heathrow Airport I joined the passport control queue. When it was my turn the immigration, officer called me and I gave him my passport. He opened it, looked at it and then glanced back at me. He looked at the form which I had filled in on the plane, giving the address and phone numbers.

The Immigration Officer asked me to stand aside and he tried to call the numbers that was written on the form which I handed to him, but all numbers were switched off. He asked me to follow him to a room which was the waiting room.

The immigration officer asked me if I had ever met these people before and what was their status in the UK. I told him that I didn't know anything about them and after an hour sitting in a waiting room, the immigration officer came and said that Tony was there to pick me up, but the immigration officer told me that he was giving me a week to leave the UK. He said that I should come back to the airport in seven days' time at 11 o'clock to return to Zimbabwe. He then escorted me to Tony.

"Hi, I am Tom and you must be Eva," Tom introduced himself. "I am sorry I was late coming to pick you up. Hope everything went well."

"Yeah, not really. I am tired. I just want and rest now," I replied.

Tom drove me to his home in Brixton. We reached the house and I met his girlfriend, who was busy preparing dinner.

"This is my girlfriend, Martha, and, Martha, meet Eva, the wife of Colonel Peter, my friend, whom I used to tell you about." Tom said.

"Oh, it's nice to meet you, Eva. You're welcome. Please sit down." Martha said warmly.

As it was freezing outside, Martha asked me if she could make me a cup of tea. While I was drinking my tea, Martha sat near me

"How was your trip, Eva?" she asked.

"Oh, I had a good flight, but I am exhausted immigration officer kept me for hours asking stupid questions," I told her.

"" What were they asking you about?" she enquired.

"They asked me about your status and if I had ever met you before. The immigration officer tried calling your phones many times but he didn't get through," I explained.

"So, what did you say about our status?" she asked.

"Nothing, because I didn't know anything and I was refused entry into the UK 'I answered'

He tried to find a seat to send me back but they couldn't find one, so they gave me one week to visit you and then I am to hand myself over to them again. I must be back at the airport by 11.30 a.m. on the 19th oh December in seven days' time to be deported to Zimbabwe. 'I explained anxiously'

"OK. Finish your tea and have a bath while I am preparing your food. You must be worn out," she said sympathetically. "These immigration officers are problems. I have never liked them," Martha said scornfully.

I finished bathing, ate my food and went straight to bed. I woke up the next day and found no one in the house. They had already gone to work, but had left a note for me. As I was too scared to go out into their town, I stayed in the house aal the times, helping Tony and Martha by doing some cooking and cleaning.

When I woke up on the 19th of December 1999, Sunday morning, it was very cold and snowing. That was my day I had to go to the airport and surrender myself to the immigration then returned to Zimbabwe.

"Good morning, Eva. What time are you supposed to be at Heathrow Airport?" Martha asked.

"Oh, I must be there by 11.30 this morning," I answered.

"OK, Tom will accompany you to the airport, he is not working today," Martha said.

"Oh, thank you very much for looking after me, but don't worry about escorting me to Heathrow. I can go by myself." I asserted bravely.

Martha, insisted that Tom should escort me to the airport and she left for work and Tom accompanied me to the railway station. We boarded a train to Heathrow, but I got off after three stops, while Tony caught some sleep. When I got out the train I looked for a phone booth and I found it then called Peter in Zimbabwe. I told him everything and he advised me not to come back because things were very bad.

I sat down on a bench and recalled all that had happened to me since I was young. I was so distressed as I didn't know where to go or what to do. I sat on that bench for almost four hours.

"Good afternoon, madam. Are you okay?" asked a man wearing a white shirt with a London Underground badge and a black trousers.

"Good afternoon. I am okay," I stammered.

"You don't look all right. You have been sitting here for almost four hours. I saw you when I started my shift and you're still sitting here looking upset."

"No, I am fine," I stuttered, as suddenly tears poured from my eyes.

"I come from Nigeria and I work for London Underground. I am married and have two children, a boy and a girl. I am not a policeman or an immigration officer. If you have a problem, tell me. I will help you if I can. Please," the man explained.

"OK. My name is Eva. What is your name?" I asked.

"Oh, sorry. My name is Chris Jacob," he answered

I told him everything and he showed great pity to me. He asked me if I wanted to go with him to his house to meet his family. At first, I was scared but had no choice because I didn't know where I would sleep that night.

Chris was six feet tall, charming and handsome. After his shift he changed into jeans and a leather jacket and drove me to his house. I was so worried that I couldn't think straight, wondering whether Chris was a genuine person or not. My heart felt as if it would break.

Chris noticed that I was not myself, so he tried to talk to me about his wife and children until we got to his home. There Chris parked his car and took my bag into the house, as I followed him.

"Darling, I am home!" Chris called.

"Hello, honey. I am upstairs. I will be down soon," his wife answered.

Chris sat me down and made me a cup of tea. His wife came down followed by her children, and was astonished to see me sitting on the sofa.

"Hello, who are you?" she asked gently.

"Oh, darling. She is Eva, our visitor. I will explain everything to you. Eva, this is my lovely wife, Emma, and these are my two children," Chris said.

"It's nice to meet you, Emma. I heard so much about you. You have beautiful kids," I murmured.

Chris took his wife upstairs and explained my story to her. Emma was tall and slim. I liked her twinkling eyes. After twenty minutes Chris and Emma came down and she made me welcome.

They lived in a detached house in Southend. It was less than a mile from the sea front and had a stunning view over the river.

I started living with the family as a maid. I looked after their children and did all the housework. Emma was not working but she spent time drinking beer and smoking like a chimney. She didn't have time for her own children nor time to cook food for her family, but depended on take-away. I started cooking for the whole family every day. I didn't get paid but in return I had food and a place to sleep.

For the first four months Emma was nice to me. I took care of the children and the house without any problem. As time went on she started treating me badly. I worked like a slave and got really tired every day. I was tired both physically and mentally, as I didn't get any time to rest.

One day I was not feeling well and I lay down. Emma entered the bedroom where I was lying and saw me there.

"Eva, you should know that you're a housemaid and should perform your duties, not lie down like a pregnant woman," she said pointedly.

"I am not feeling good. I just want to rest for a few hours, then I will start doing my work," I replied.

"If you don't do your work, my dear, I will throw you back out into the street," she said.

Chris didn't know what was happening because he spent most of his time at work and, when he was off duty, he went out with his friends.

I spent another seven months living with them as a prisoner and I had achieved nothing. I didn't have freedom to say or do anything on my own. If there is no freedom, happiness there is no life.

One Friday night on the 25th of November, Emma went out with her friends and Chris was also gone - he used to go out for the whole weekend the last week of every month.

I did all my housework, fed the children and put them to bed. I couldn't sleep that night because the house was very cold. I didn't know that Emma had switched off the heater which was in the room which I was sleeping. With no heating I sat up, was devastated. So, in the middle of the night I picked up the phone and rang 'Peter'.

"Hello, who is this?" Peter answered.

"I am your wife, Eva," I stammered.

I spent almost twenty minutes telling my Peter, how I was suffering and said that I wanted to come home.

"Things are not good here, Eva. I am being targeted by the government, as my workmates and my superiors discovered that you're in the UK, and you are the supporter of the opposite party. So please, don't come. It's not safe for you," he explained.

"I heard all that you said, but I have suffered enough. I want to come home. I miss my children, so much / most of all too," I replied.

"The children are all okay and they're missing you too. I will phone you when I get a chance. Bye!" he concluded.

"Hello, hello!" I called out, as I sat with the phone against my ear, listening to an empty, humming noise. I put the phone back and went back to sit on the bed.

The following morning of 26th of November 2000 at five am. I heard the noise of the door and it was Emma entering the house, drunk and puffing away on a cigarette. She looked at me and burst out laughing.

I looked at her and asked if she was ok, but continued laughing.

"What is your problem?" she asked, still laughing.

"No problem," I sighed.

She dropped herself on the sofa and started yawning. I took off her shoes and covered her with a duvet, after taking the cigarette from her mouth. I was so angry that I went upstairs and packed my bag. I had two dresses, one coat, two pairs of trousers and two pairs of trainers. I didn't do any housework that day. Instead, I sat downstairs and waited for Emma to wake up. She woke up around 10 a.m. and asked me if I had prepared food as usual, but I told her that I hadn't touched anything in the house that morning.

When Emma heard me say that, she became furious with me.

"So why are you sitting down there, staring at me and doing nothing?" Emma asked angrily.

"I was waiting for you to wake up. Thank you for all you have done for me. I have decided to go back to Zimbabwe. I will surrender myself at the police station and the police will know what to do. I want to go home," I explained with resignation / determination)

Emma took a cigarette from the box, lit it, and blew out a cloud of smoke from her cigarette. There was a long pause while she stared at me, totally astonished.

"Bye, Emma. Tell your husband and your lovely children that I have gone," I gasped.

I grabbed my bag, gripped the door handle and pushed the door open.

The police station was only twenty minutes' walk from Chris and Emma's house. I got there around 11.30 in the morning.

"Good morning, madam. How can I help you?" the police officer asked.

"Good morning, sir. I have come to surrender myself to you. I want to go back to my country, Zimbabwe. I am illegally in this country." I announced hesitantly.

"Oh, sit down. Someone will take care of you."

Another policeman came and took me inside. He took my name and asked the date I came to the UK. They called Immigration and arranged everything to transport me to the airport. I was at the police from the time I arrived till 3pm

I was taken from the police station at 3.30 pm to Heathrow Airport by two men in a nice car and we reached the airport that Saturday evening at five o'clock.

I was given a comfortable seat, and, after an hour's wait, I was escorted by an immigration officer on board a Zimbabwe Airways plane and left the UK at nine pm that night, on the 26th of November 2000.

I was very excited that I was going to be reunited with my family. I didn't know that the night I had spoken to my Peter, my husband, was the day he had been taken away by Mugabe's central intelligence people. None of his family knew where he was, he had disappeared.

I reached Zimbabwe the next morning at 6.30am on the 27th of November 2000. The plane landed, the passengers got off one by one, and I followed. I saw two men waiting near the plane and, when I had come down the steps, they asked me if I was Eva Kupa, wife of Colonel Kupa

"Yes, I am," I answered.

"Can you come with us?" one of them requested brusquely.

I followed them past the immigration control and the customs, and went straight into an office, where a woman and three men were sitting.

"Do you know why you're in this office?" the woman asked.

"No, I don't know," I answered.

"OK, we want to ask you some few questions about your journey to the UK," she explained.

I was seated on a chair near one man and facing other three men sitting. These three men were looking very smart wearing grey suits, white shirts and black shoes. Three of them started asking me questions one by one which I didn't understand. After an hour they showed me a paper which accused me of being a traitor. I was shocked, but was then told that I was going to be taken to the Central Police station for more questioning.

I was driven to there by a uniformed police officer and there were other two men waiting for me. When I got inside the police station, I was told to take off my shoes, belt. The uniformed police officer searched me thoroughly and I was placed in a small, stinking, underground cell where there was a very dim light but I couldn't see anything. I thought that maybe there had been some mistake but I realised that it was really happening to me. I spent the whole day and night in that cell.

The next day at 10 a.m. on the 28th of November 2000, the police officer let me out of the cell. I was taken to another office, where I found two men, one in uniform and the other in plain clothes, waiting to interrogate me.

"Do you know why you were arrested yesterday, madam?" the man in plain clothes asked.

"No, I was told that I was going to be asked a few questions, but I am surprised to find myself in a cell," I lamented with tears in my eyes.

They asked me questions in turns for about one hour. I was tired and I hadn't had anything to eat or drink since the previous day. One of the police women came with a cup of tea and a piece of bread, and gave them to me. I drank two sips of tea, but couldn't eat the bread because I was too overwrought, feeling confused and threatened.

I was put back into the cell for about an hour, and then the police woman came back to drag me off to another big room. There I was told to take off my clothes, she flogged my buttocks. I screamed for help but there was no help. I regretted coming back to Zimbabwe. If I had listened to Peter, none of this would be happening. I cried and cried but no one heard me. Some of the police officers were even laughing.

After some minutes of torture, I was released on condition that I should report to the nearest police station once a week. I walked out of the station in pain and I saw a bus stop one hundred metres away, so I sat down there on a bench to think where to go and what to do. I was empty, tired and terrified.

While I was sitting thinking, people were passing and buses were coming and going. I rested my chin on my knees and, when I lifted my head up again, I saw a woman walking past the bus stop.

"Excuse me, can you help me, please?" I asked politely.

The woman stopped and I greeted her in our traditional way: "Makadii zvenyu?" (How are you, mother?) As she returned the greeting, she paused for a long time, while she stared at me closely.

"Are you Eva?" she asked.

"Yes, I am Eva, and who are you?" I whispered.

"I am Noma. We used to live in the same village, but when you dropped out of school, I was sent to boarding school, so we never met again," she explained. "Oh, it's a long time, my dear. We were still young that time. You look distressed and tired, are you all right?" she asked. I didn't answer her, instead I asked her if she was married. She answered that she got married but the marriage didn't work.

"I met your cousin, Tanya, two months ago. I didn't recognise her, but she knew me and introduced herself. Your sister told me that you had got married and that your husband had sent you to the UK. When did you come back?"

"I came back yesterday. I was in custody, accused of betraying the country to the British. I am tired, scared and in pain. I don't know what to do, Norma, or where to go. Please, help," I pleaded, with tears in my eyes.

"No, don't worry. I will take you to your cousin sister's house. I know where she lives. We were good kids when we were young, and I can be always here for you," Norma said.

Noma went to collect her car from where it was parked, and drove me to my cousin sister Tanya, On our way to Tanya's house, I explained a little what had happened in

UK and on arrival in Zimbabwe to Noma. Tanya lived five miles outside the city and was a nurse, working at a nearby clinic. She was still single and had no children.

When we got to my Tanya's home, Noma got out of the car to check to see if Tanya was in. Noma knocked on the door and Tanya opened it. It was around six in the evening.

"Oh, surprise, hello stranger meaning Noma. What's brought you to my house at this time of the night?" Tanya asked.

"I have a visitor for you, Tanya. Hope you're fine," Noma added.

"Oh, who is this visitor? I will leave the door open," Tanya said.

Noma came back to the car and helped me to get out of the car, I was in a lot of pain and struggled to walk into the house as my buttocks were very painful.

My cousin sister Tanya was in the kitchen when we entered the house. She heard the noise of the door and she knew that we had arrived.

"I am coming. Make yourself comfortable. I will be with you shortly," Tanya said, as she came out of the kitchen and saw me.

'Eva, you're back. I am happy to see you, but you don't look well. Are you all right?" she asked with concern

"She is not fine, Tanya. Do you have something for pain? she is in pain," Noma explained.

"Oh, I have some strong painkillers" Tanya said, and she quickly rushed to get them. "What exactly has happened to you, Eva?

Have you had an accident?" Tanya gasped through tears, as she could see that I was in suffering greatly.

Norma gave Tanya a knowing look and shook her head.

"I don't think she can talk now, Tanya. Let's leave it until tomorrow," Noma said.

"Just give me something to eat and then I will take the painkillers, as I want to rest," I requested"

"Your children are sleeping in the bedroom. Their father left them here with me soon after you left for England, and he has never come to see them as we didn't want the children to be in trouble. I'm sure you would like to see them," Tanya said.

"If they are okay, I will see them tomorrow. I don't want them to see me in this state," I said. I was so grieved to hear that my husband had never come back for the children. I had two bites of a sandwich and took the painkillers for the pain, which soon began to ease. I slept in the lounge and woke up the following morning at 4 a.m. I couldn't get back to sleep because of pains, I was experiencing.

My children woke up at 6 a.m. and came to the lounge to clean the floor, dirty plates in the kitchen and tidy up furniture before leaving for school. When my daughter saw me sitting on the sofa in the lounge, she threw the sweeping broom away, and she shouted, "Mummy, mummy, when did you come?"

"I came last night," I answered.

"Tony and Tody come and see mummy. She is back!" Lisa, my daughter shouted, she was now fourteen years

My two sons came running from the bedroom and wanted to jump on me but I stopped them.

"Why, mummy, don't you love me anymore?" Lisa, Tony and Tody asked.

"I love you so much and I have missed you my children. It's only that I am not feeling well."

They sat down beside me and I kissed them on the cheeks. I was delighted to be reunited with my children and see them in good health.

They didn't want to go to school that day, but my Tanya persuaded them to go and drove off with them to drop them at school.

Tanya came straight back after taking them to school. She cooked corn porridge for me and I ate few spoons of porridge. Tanya and Noma were sitting beside me while I was eating and when I had finished eating, I took the pain killers. Tanya and Noma were curios to hear what had had happened to me.

'Eva', tell me what happened to you? "Tanya asked" I then explained what had happened to me, Tanya and Noma were both aghast.

Tanya wept and looked wretched she then said, you are lucky Eva, these people are dangerous you could have been killed or disappear without trace. The police and soldiers are supposed to protect people but there are forced to kill innocent people, and abusing their powers.

People are kidnapped, tortured and by Mugabe's people if they are suspected to be against the government "Noma added"

What has happen had happened, and let's not keep talking about it because we don't know who is listening. I do not want to put you people and myself in trouble again, "
"I spoke"

Tanya assisted me with bathing as it was difficult for me to do it myself, and told me that she was going to take me to the doctors before the children come home from school,"

Noma left for her house that morning and promised to come back after some days to check on me. Tanya took me to their doctor's as we arrived at the doctors, Tanya asked the nurse to speak with her in private as it was my first time to be at that doctor's surgery. After the nurse spoke with Tanya, the nurse went to talk with the doctor and after about twenty minutes I was called in.

The doctor asked me what had happened, and I told him what had happened and showed no surprise and he was coming across with people in these situations and were even worse than mine. He instructed the nurse to give me some medication and an injection.

After being treated and given my medication, we left for Tanya's house. When we arrived home, Tanya made some cups of tea and started telling me about the disappearance of Peter.

Your husband Peter disappeared because he was against of killing and torturing innocent people. He was forced to be one of those officers who were appointed to be involved in torturing and interrogating innocent people, whom they suspected were against the government. "Tanya explained"

Do you mean Peter my husband was now a murderer that he goes around killing innocent people?" I asked

"No" I didn't mean that, but I want you to know that he was asked to be involved and he was against the whole situation. "Tanya explained"

So what am I going to do, if these people know that I am back, they will kill me and my children," I exclaimed.

These people are wicked and look at what they have done to you. This is a warning of life or death. We should do something quickly, as soon as you're feeling better. "Tanya explained anxiously.

After an hour, children came back from school and the house throbbed with noise and it became untidy. My children were very happy to see me in the house.

Tanya's house was a three bedroomed house with a black gate at the front. I stayed indoors for almost two weeks recovering from my beatings. I started moving around the house and in the garden, when I started feeling better.

We had good Christmas together with the children, Tanya and Noma though we didn't have much. We spent our Christmas day indoors. Tanya slaughtered a big chicken and Noma helped Tanya to cook rice and chicken. We all sat down with my three children as a family and ate together. It meant everything that as I was happy to see my children safe and my cousin Tanya.

We celebrated the new year in 2001 without any problem, we were always indoors and we could the neighbours shouting for happy new but we couldn't do because of the fear of zanu pf people. After new year in February I could feel that I was recovered but living in fear all the days thinking that these Mugabe's people could visit me anytime if they know that about me. So I was thinking of travelling to Mozambique where my brother had migrated. I wanted to go with my children and join my brother as I feel safe in that country.

One Sunday on the 18th of February 2001, around seven pm. I was sitting on the balcony resting my elbow on the window sill, starring out of the window and watching the dusky darken sky.

I could hear the noise of people singing coming from the main road.

Suddenly, without warning I heard people at the gate singing and shouting, throwing stones and demanding to be let into the house.

"Mother, did you hear the noise? Lisa, my daughter asked.
"Yes I heard the noise, please go to your bedroom kids and stay calm. I think they are just people singing. I explained carefully. I didn't want my children to be frightened and I knew these people had come to cause trouble.

"Why are these people making such noise? Are they not Mugabe's people mum? I hate them, Lisa whispered through tears.

Don't worry Lisa, maybe they want us to go to their meeting. Just take your brother to the bedroom I will take care of the situation, I explained hopefully.

While I was talking to Lisa, the crowd was forcing itself into the yard. From the window I could see people clambering over the high wall to break open the gate. My heart started pounding as I knew they had come for trouble. I was worried about the survival of my children and my cousin sister Tanya, she was only person I had left with, my children and my brother Brighton who was now living in Mozambique.

The crowd managed to enter in the premises and started shouting, singing liberation songs. I couldn't do anything but remained sitting, it was very scary

A tall man walked towards where I was sitting and screamed to me asking if I had come to collect more information for Blair.

Tanya had gone to bed early that day because she has been tired, but she was woken up by the noise.

There is no one collecting the information for Ton's Blair from this house. Tanya answered from nowhere.

Where There Is No Freedom or Peace There Is No Life

I am not talking to you I am looking for the spy who just came from Tony's Blair country: he "spouted nastily"

If you are looking for me I am here but am not a spy, "I shouted"

After shouted the man confronted me and gave me a sharp slap, I didn't move or slap him back but I asked him, why he slapped me. He answered that because he wanted to, then I said thank you.

He then said you are very stubborn and I want to teach you a lesson. He was holding a stick in his right hand, he started hitting me with that stick: calling me a spy. He was just hitting me hard every part of my body and while he was hitting me, one woman came and drove her fist under my chin and I fall down. The impact made me to cry loud in pain and I tried to get up but I was in a rage by then.

The children heard the noise of my cry, and the ran to the lounge where these people were harassing me and Tanya.

"When they saw me knocked down and bleeding, they started crying and shouting for help. The woman kept on punching me and Tanya jumped on her and dragged her down. I managed to wake up, sat down but was unconscious didn't know what was happening. After some minutes I became conscious and looked around to check if my children were not hate.

When those people realised that they could have killed Tanya, they disappeared one by one soon only I remained there with my children and Tanya lying on the floor facing down. I looked from where I was sitting and saw her head in a pool of blood, and I could also hear the noise of the crowd and saw people run off the house.

I looked at the clock on the wall but couldn't see the time, as it was dark. I struggled to stand up and managed to stand up. I took the children into their bedroom, my children were shaking and crying, so I hugged them and tried to calm them. I returned to Tanya with a blanket and cover her as I thought she was cold.

I didn't know what to do, I couldn't think straight so I took Tanya's phone and dialled the last number which was Noma. This was late, I guess Noma had already gone to bed and faster asleep. Noma didn't answer so I hanged the call.

After twenty minutes, Tanya's phone rang, so I picked it up, it was Norma.

Hello Tanya sorry I missed your call

How are you and how is Eva?" she asked.

Noma was concerned about me more because she that I could be in trouble anytime with this people of Zanu PF.

We are all fine, thank you," I answered with a low voice.

Tanya, you sound low. Is Eva okay?" Noma enquired.

"It's me Eva Noma, Tanya is not well this side; I responded.

Those people visited us today and hurt Tanya.

I don't know what to do now," I muttered through my tears.

"Eva, where is Tanya? Noma inquired

She is lying on the floor; "I answered"

"Ok I am coming now Eva, "Noma confirmed"

I don't think it is a good idea for you to come over, because you might get in trouble too." I told her.

Noma didn't listen and within an hour she had arrived at Tanya's house.

Noma entered the house, looked at where I was, and she found me sitting beside Tanya in the pool of blood: sobbing silently and was not thinking straight and had no idea what to do next.

Noma She then got me to my feet and took me to the bathroom, where she turned on the shower for me. I washed off all the blood and soaked my dress in a basin.

Did you phone the ambulance to take Tanya to hospital Eva?" Noma asked

"No, I didn't know what to do. I'm confused, Noma."

"Okay, Eva. Let me phone them."

When she phoned the ambulance, she was told that they were short of ambulances, so there was nothing they could do.

Noma decided to take Tanya to hospital in her car by herself and left us behind.

When she got to the hospital, Noma was told that Tanya lost a lot of blood and she was dead.

After hearing that Tanya was dead, Noma drove back to Tanya's house where she left us and this was around midnight. This was the darkest night for my children and myself though I had survived the liberation war. I asked myself that is this what is called liberation, and I answered myself no, it's not liberation.

When she got home, I was sitting on the chair in dark waiting to hear what she was going to say about Tanya.

I asked if Tanya was admitted at the hospital as she was unconscious but didn't want to say much but to say Tanya is in good hands.

"I think it would be best for us to leave this house because those people might come back again," Noma warned.

"Do you have your brother's phone number in Mozambique," Noma asked.

"I think I can get the number from Tanya's phone," I said.

Noma took a torch from her car, switched on and gave it to me. I looked in the phone book and found the number and I gave it to Noma.

She called my brother and told him everything and he also advised us to leave the house.

My children came out of their bedroom when they heard me talking to Noma, they were sobbing silently with tears of anger, shame and hurt. They asked if they would go to see their aunt Tanya at hospital.

I told them that they would go to see their aunt in hospital when things are calm. I didn't know what else to tell them. After twenty minutes I pulled myself together enough to tell my children that we should leave the house.

All the windows were broken, the decorations destroyed, the whole house smashed. It was as if someone had taken all my emotions away, locked them up and I felt nothing. I looked at my children and Noma, but just couldn't say anything.

"Where are we going?" Lisa asked.

"We are going to my aunt's place in the countryside," I answered politely.

Eva, let me drive you and the children to your aunt's village and I should come cack as soon as I drop you safely "Noma offered"

My aunt lived in a remote village, and it was two hours' drive to reach it from where Tanya lived. Noma packed a bag and put the children in the car.

We left Tanya's house on the early hours of the 19th of February Monday at about 4 a.m. and reached my aunt's village at 6 o'clock in the morning and my aunt was already awake sweeping her yard.

When my aunt saw the car stopping at her yard, she stopped sweeping to see who was visiting her that early morning.

Noma parked the car, got out then met my aunty and greeted her in our language. Noma introduced herself and told my aunt that she had brought me and my children, as things were not okay.

Noma and my aunt never met before and she thought it was someone who came to buy chickens as she used to breed chickens and keep the for business.

Then, wasting no time, Noma picked up the bag and got the children out of the car. My aunt opened another the door where I was sitting, she holds my hand and assisted me to get out of the car. I was in pain because of the floggings which I had received from these Mugabe people so my body was very painful

Aunt asked what was the problem as I was not looking good.

"I am fine, aunt. Let's go inside, please, and I will explain everything to you. I said.

"Okay," she agreed. "Let me help you inside the house."

Once we were all in the house, my aunt began questioning me anxiously.

"Eva, is everything okay? What brought you here in this condition? Did your husband beat you?"

"No, aunty. I don't even know where my husband is, Tanya is dead. She was killed yesterday by Mugabe's people," I said softly through tears.

"Oh, my God! Why did they kill her? What terrible thing had she done?" my aunt begged.

"She did nothing, aunty," I replied and explained the whole story to her.

My aunty was touched and became emotional, she started sobbing silently for almost an hour and she was tired.

"Aunt, stop. Look the children are crying, too. What has happened, has happened. Let's think of what to do now." I said.

"Okay, I hear you," she said as she wiped her tears and gave my children some cooked peanuts to eat.

"I don't know what to do aunt, my life is empty. I don't want to end up in trouble again," I explained.

"I heard all that you told me and what happened to you when you were in England. You came back for your children, but it's not safe for you and your children anymore.

We have to think and do something fast," my aunt said.

"I don't know what to do, aunt, and I am so confused. Tanya is lying in the mortuary now because of me. Help me, aunt," I pleaded.

"Okay, give me time to think out a solution to this mess," she replied.

She prepared food and helped me to bathe. I couldn't eat much as my mind was to Tanya, I took my tablets and slept, I needed to rest my head.

The children, too, quickly went to sleep, as none of us had slept the previous night. My aunt spent the whole day monitoring me and the children because we were traumatised.

The next day on the 21st of February 2001, my aunt left for Bindura to organise a passport under a different name. Bindura was the nearest small town, fifteen miles from my aunt's village. When she came back in the evening she told me that everything was done and I had to sign the passport form and give them my photo.

"How did you do all this without me, aunt?" I asked.

"Eva, if you have the money in this country, you can get what you want. You can bribe anyone to get what you need in minutes. The government is not paying people well, so they will do anything to survive," my aunt explained.

As it was already night, my aunt prepared supper. We all ate and then went to sleep in the kitchen. The following day on the 22nd of February 2002 my aunt's friend's son, who worked at the passport office, came and drove us to Bindura and I had my passport photo taken. It didn't look much like me because my eyes were still a little swollen because of crying. I handed in my picture and signed the passport form. Within thirty minutes I was given my passport. I couldn't believe it and I thought I was dreaming, but it was real.

"Thank you very much, aunt, but what am I going to do with this passport? I don't have money to travel anywhere," I said dejectedly.

"Don't worry Eva, and leave everything to me. I will do my best to save your life. Remember my daughter and son are based in South Africa. I will talk to them tonight," my aunt said.

My aunt was not really old, only about sixty. Her husband had been killed during the liberation war and she was left with a son and a daughter. She kept a herd of cattle and goats; She also breed chickens and sell them. She was well-known because she helped with the cooking and laundry at the local orphanage.

The same evening of 22nd of February, that we came back from collecting the passport, my aunt phoned her daughter, Samantha, who was single and working in Johannesburg as a social worker. When my aunt had finished explaining everything to Samantha, she came inside the house where I was lying down.

"I am going to see a butcher to ask him if he wants to buy some cattle. He buys livestock to slaughter and sells the meats. He pays good money, especially for cows," my aunt told me.

"What did your daughter say, aunt?" I asked.

"Everything is under control. We will be leaving for South Africa the day after tomorrow in the evening," my aunt announced.

My aunt went to see the butcher man the following morning of the 23rd of February 2001 and came back happy with a wad of money.

"I sold two cows and he paid me cash. He will collect the cows in the evening."

My aunt didn't rest that day, went to organise some transport with one of the man, who was a teacher at the nearest school.

We left for South Africa the after a day on the 25th of February 2001 in the evening. It took us one and a half days to reach Johannesburg. When we got there, it was in the afternoon of the 27th of February 2001, everybody was exhausted and I was in very severe pain.

The man who had driven us to Johannesburg was paid his money and he drove off back to Zimbabwe the next day on the 29th of February 2001 after he had a good rest.

When my aunt's daughter saw the way I was looking, she immediately took me to hospital, I was admitted and stayed there for a week.

After I came out I was much better and stayed at Samantha's house for another week, as she and my aunt wanted me to recuperate.

I was very pleased to be able to spend time with my children, although I was not fully fit.

The third week my aunt told me that I would be leaving for the UK in two days.

"Aunt, I don't know anyone in the UK. I don't think I can go back to Chris and Emma's house again. Am I not safe here in South Africa?" I asked.

"No, you're not safe here. I want you to go far away. Samantha has arranged everything with a friend, who works in the UK as a nurse.

She has agreed to take care of you until you settle," my aunt explained.

"If you say so, aunt. I believe what you say and I put my trust in you," I acknowledged.

I thanked Samantha for all the help she had given me, and gave warm thanks to my aunt.

In the evening of 4th April 2001, I boarded a British Airways flight to London from South Africa.

I reached in the UK, the following morning the 5th of April 2001 around eight am. I went through immigration control, submitted my passport and was given a visitor's visa for six months without any problem.

After I had gone through customs, I collected my suitcase and went straight to the exit as I didn't have anything to declare. I looked around and saw a woman waving a board with my name on it, and I knew right away that she was Samantha's friend, Pola. I went straight over to her.

"You must be Eva," she announced.

"Yes, I am Eva, and you must be Pola, Samantha's friend."

"Yes, I am Pola." Welcome to our cold country she said with a smile on her face.

She grabbed my suitcase and walked to the car park, unlock her car with a remote key and put the suitcase in the boot. She opened the passenger door and asked me to enter in the car and she also enter the car on the driver's seat then drove me to her home in Brighton. On our way to Brighton we were chatting like we had met before. Pola was bright in complexion, dark brown eyes, curly hair and she was tall, slim and beautiful. She was a socialise person and cheerful, so it didn't take me time to engage with her. It took three hours to get there from Heathrow because of traffic.

When we got home in Brighton, Pola parked the car and took out the suitcase from the boot. She unlocked the front door, and we entered the house.

When we were in the house, I asked Pola if I could use her phone to call South Africa. I was anxious to tell my aunt that I had reached safety, thanks to everything she and her daughter had done for me.

Aunt stayed in South Africa for another week and returned to Zimbabwe on the 14th of April 2001 with my children. It was reassuring that my children were safe in my aunt's home.

After a week being in UK, one Pola came from work and sat on the chair looking very tired. She asked me to make her a cup of tea and I did. After she had rested she told me that there was a vacancy of a cleaner at the local hospital where she was working as a nurse.

Those years it was not difficult to get a job or open an account. The following day, Pola gave me the phone number without delay to phone and I did call the number at 08:30.

I was invited for an interview the following day at 2pm. I informed Pola about the interview and told her that I was nervous to be interviewed about the job as I never worked before, and this was my first interview.

The most thing which was making me nervous was to be interviewed with white person, but Pola told me to be confident and started couching pretending like she was interviewing me. She was asking me questions and taught how to respond to the interviewer, have eye contact.

Pola has worked as a cleaner when she first came to UK and later trained to become a nurse. So, she had full knowledge of the job description,

The next day I went to the interview and I was late with ten minutes. I met a tall white, slim woman. She asked me to sit down and offered me a cup of tea.

She asked my first name and last name. I answered her with a smile.

She then asked me if I had experience. I answered "yes' with confidence.

She then asked me If I could start the following morning at 7am. She also asked me to bring an ID, passport, driver's licence, or birth certificate.

I could not believe it, that I got a job and I was so happy and went back home.

When I got home from the interview, I prepared dinner because Pola was going to be home from work at 6pm.

Pola got home and I couldn't wait, I shouted as soon as she opened the door and informed her about the job. She was happy for me, and she went straight to her bedroom, changed the uniform, and had shower. She put on pyjamas, headed downstairs and we had dinner together.

I got a job working as a cleaner, worked six days in a week and had one day off. I got paid every week and contributed few pounds for rent and help to buy some of the groceries once in a month. Most of the things Pola was doing by herself because she had a well-paid job.

Pola encouraged me to save money from my wages, so I could buy tickets for my children to join me in UK.

While in the process of arranging my children to join me, I received a phone call from Zimbabwe to tell me that my daughter had been raped by Mugabe's people. This call was made by aunt as she was very ashamed thinking, I was going to be made with her.

I did understand what these Mugabe's people were like. I tried my best to calm myself when my aunt delivered that sad news to me, I told her to hang on the phone and promised to call her back which I never did. I didn't call her back because I didn't want to put her trouble, as we didn't know who could listen to the conversation and end up in the hands of the enemies.

My daughter was only fourteen years going to fifteen years. I was distraught, so I called Samantha in South Africa.

I asked, if she knew what had happened to my daughter Lisa and said her mother my aunt had told her, and she was trying to find out a way of bringing them back to South Africa.

I asked her if she could go to Zimbabwe to get my children and take them back to South Africa and stay with her for the time being as I was saving some money to bring them and join me in UK. She agreed and I sent the money, which I had saved from working for the last eight months.

Instead of her going she sent the money to aunt her mother and asked her to travel to South Africa with my children. My aunt agreed and this time she flew to South Africa instead of hiring someone to drive them.

My children arrived in South Africa safely accompanied with my aunt and stayed at Samantha 'house for another two weeks with my aunt as Samantha was working full time at the hospital.

On Wednesday the 17th of October 2001, Samantha called me, informing me that I should go to Gatwick airport and meet my children as she and my aunt had organised everything from passport to their journey to UK.

This didn't surprise me as I knew that my aunt could do anything for my children to be safe.

Lisa, Tony and Tody arrived in UK on the 19th of October 200, It was not easy for me to get my children from the hands of Immigration.

When my children arrived at Gatwick airport. They were refused entry in the UK though I was waiting for them.

The children waited for more than six hours in one of the rooms being asked some questions with the immigration officer. I was worried because the flight had arrived at 08:00 am.

The immigration was worried that Lisa, Tony and Tody were underage, and were holding Zimbabwe passports but they were coming from South Africa, so they involved social workers.

I waited at the Exit almost six hours, I headed to the information desk and asked the woman who was sitting behind the desk. The woman was so helpful, she made a phone call and was informed that the children were held inside with the immigration under investigations.

The immigration was informed that the mother was waiting for them at the exit ready to meet them. After ten minutes one of the immigration officers came to pick me from the information desk.

He asked me to follow him and he took me where the children were. I met my children looked very tired, but they were looked after very well.

One of the social worker was sitting with them, and I was happy to see them health, I was taken to another room with one of the immigration officer.

The officer sat me down, offered me a cup of tea. She started interviewing about my status in UK. I didn't waste time but told her the truth that my stay was expired, I explained everything what had happened back in Zimbabwe, and what made me to come to UK, also why I have decided to bring my children to join in UK.

The immigration was touched with the story and she advised me to seek asylum after narrating my story to her.

We were taken in a temporary accommodation in Essex and after two weeks were given a house and some money for food every week.

After some days I was advised by the social worker to register with a doctors near where we were staying. I took my children to the doctors' for a check-up and delivered that my daughter was pregnant as a result of the rape.

I would have taken her to hospital for an abortion, but she was by then four months pregnant, so we decided to keep the baby. She gave birth to a beautiful baby girl on 26th of April 2002, and she called her Tanya. My daughter was then granted one year and was allocated a flat hundred metres from where we were staying. When she left for her new accommodation with her daughter, I was left behind with my two sons.

These two boys were still young, nine years and eleven years. As the years passed by, my sons were growing up every day like they were being put fertilizer. They looked like twins only that the younger son is tall and built like with powerful muscles, born more physical

The older son is stunningly, full sensuous lips guaranteed to drive girls wild.

My sons were not happy and were affected in a way that, they were not entitled for anything because of their status. Life became unfair for them as they needed some pocket money to school.

The money we were receiving for upkeeping was very small and only afford to buy food, pay bills such as electricity, gas, water and help my sons with their transport to school.
I couldn't manage to celebrate my son's birthdays or buy them gifts. At Christmas we were not be able to celebrate as others were doing and we treated that Christmas as a normal day.

After a year I went to court in Croydon for a hearing of my asylum claim, and it was refused. And the solicitor appealed against the decision, but It was still refused asylum.

The government kept supporting me and my children, but we were not allowed to work or to study, further to University level.

We have been in the UK for seven years now, with no papers, no freedom and no peace of mind. Where there is no freedom, happiness and peace of mind, there is no life.

Having living in this country all those years, I have come to realise when I was living in Zimbabwe: I never had to think about identity and the privileges that I used to have I used to take them for granted.

For instance, when I was growing, I never needed to think about any skin colour as everyone around me was black and spoke the same language as a result we all shared the norms and values.

Being in this country as black woman, I have become aware of what it means to be black living in a white dominated country regardless of all what other cultures or race call me. I also learned to identify myself as a black woman and believed in myself no matter what other people think of me and my children.

My son finished primary and enrolled to secondary school. At those seven years we have moved to four houses and my children had moved to three schools and became very difficult to make friends.

My elder son finished her secondary and he passed his GSEC very well. He got a place at Civic College in Benfleet and he left his younger brother behind at the secondary school to finish his GSEC.

My son started experiencing bullying from other students, and it became an intensive year for him. He was being called all sorts of names but he was very brave at the beginning. After six months he couldn't bare it anymore. My son became aggressive and isolated. I could see that my son's behaviour had changed. I asked him so many times if something was worrying him, but he kept on saying he was alright

It was on Friday the 11th of May 2007 around twelve in the afternoon, I had just come from the shops. My mobile phone rang with a private number

Hello good afternoon madam

Good afternoon, Who is this?

I'm Mr Evans calling from Chaveldon school, can I speak with Ms Kura.

Yes, it is Ms Kura, is everything alright?

There is problem between Toddy and one of the students: and I am asking you to come to school immediately Please.

Ok, I will there in twenty minutes.

I locked the door and walked to the bus station. Fortunately, the bus arrived within five minutes, and I boarded the bus to the school. The bus took about fifteen minutes to get where I was dropped.

I started walking towards school which was fifty miles from the bus stop, I entered the school yard through a small gate which was designed for visitors. I went straight to the reception and saw a woman who was sitting behind the desk. I introduced myself and straight away she took me to the room where my son was sitting with a female teacher.

The female teacher greeted me with cheerful and I greeted back. Toddy looked closed to tears which he couldn't take and the female teacher explained to me what had happened between Toddy my son and another student.

I looked at my son for a long time, saying nothing but allowing the pity to seep through my body together with my feeling that it was not my son's fault. For all that bravado and attitude, he was still a sensitive young boy. I reached over his hand, and I waited a bit and took a deep breath and went for it.

What happened Toddy? I asked politely, my son gave me one of his glances, bright eyes lowered. He looked at me hard once again

I'm sorry mum; he stammered.

I took my son home, he went straight to sleep in one of the bedrooms and refused to eat. The brother came back from college and I asked him to give his young brother space as he had a long day at school. So the older brother slept on the sofa as they didn't have their own bedrooms but shared one.

The next day was Saturday and everybody was home. I made our traditional porridge with peanut butter for breakfast. My sons loved our traditional food so much so I cooked for them that Saturday evening. After having our dinner at around six pm, they cleaned the plates, and cleared the house.

I sat down with my sons, switched off the TV and I spoke to my children advised them that not to argue with people and also not to compare themselves with others as it will make them unhappy in life and not archive their goals. I explained to them that there is always some-one better than them, but in themselves was the best thing no-matter what other people think about them. I always told my children to let go, what they cannot control. Toddy my younger son promised that he will not involve himself in any troubles until he finishes his GSCE.

At this time my sons were sharing one bedroom, so the older son slept where ever he happened to fall asleep each night, which was usually on the sofa. Seeing all these things happening to my sons, I suffered sadness and finds life more struggle for me and the boys and another part of my mind was happy because we were in a safe country.

Since my son Toddy had been involved in fighting with another student, he didn't want to go back so he was home for two weeks and I could understand him. I informed the school about the situation

After two weeks the school headmaster called and asked If Toddy could come back to school. Toddy didn't want to go back to the same school, he feared getting himself into the trouble again with other students.

After I and his older spoke to him for the second time. He later agreed to go back to school and finish his GSCE, Toddy passed all the subjects and joined his brother Tony at the college for his 'A' levels. My elder son was only left with another year to finish and looking forward to start University.

Tony the elder son finished his 'A' levels the following year and left the college leaving his younger brother Tody behind again. At this time Tody was not bullied and he was at the college for another year after Tony left and seemed happy

Tony my elder son started applying for a place to different universities and he was offered a place at Kingstone University. The administrating departing asked him to bring an ID for the form of a passport or any other document which shows that he has been granted visa and he could study in UK without restrictions.

Tony could not provide any document as we were still waiting for the decision from the Home Office. He became very distressed about the situation, and this made him very unhappy that he was not going further with his education and become what he wanted to be.

I also became depressed knowing that my sons could not go further to university because of our status.

It was in June 2009, my son Tony came from collecting his results at college and he had passed very well. He sat down on the sofa in the sitting room looking unhappy and I could see that my son was not happy, though he had passed his "A" levels. Tony has been given a deadline at Kingston University to produce the requested information.

I asked Tony, if he was ok?

Tony sighed, and answered me with teary eyes saying Mum, I passed my college but I cannot go further with my education. I cannot fulfil my dream, what I want is to go to University and graduate like other children but I cannot do it because of a paper called visa mum.

I looked at him, and told him everything will be fine and you are going to University, it might not be this year but you are definitely going to University son.

Ok mum let me go inside the bedroom, I want to rest my head, He said

In 2009 on the 25th of June, It was Thursday around ten in the morning, I was lying on top of the bed reflecting on what had happened back in Zimbabwe which led us to come to UK. This was a big picture of my life and darkest moment, but always felt life would get better one day. I heard a door bell and I quickly got up and headed downstairs and opened the door.

I saw the post man standing at the door holding a big brown envelope.

'Good morning, madam' post man said

Good morning, Sir; is this our post? I asked

Yes, but I need to see your ID, He asked

Oh sure, give me a minute; I then ran upstairs to collect my asylum card and brought it downstairs where the postman was standing waiting for the ID.

I handed over the ID to the postman and he checked the ID he asked me to sign and he handover the envelope over to me and he left.

I closed the door and dropped the envelope on top of the table downstairs without opening it. I went back upstairs to lie back in bed.

After an hour I got up and had shower, I then went downstairs straight to the Kitchen, put the kettle on and made a cup of coffee. I sat down on the sofa and sipped my coffee. I then glanced on the table where I dropped the envelope. I noticed that the envelope was addressed to my name.

I then opened the envelope and discovered that there were some passports inside the envelope and a written letter.

It took me about five minutes to open the letter as I thought our application has been refused again.

I finally opened it and started reading, the letter was telling me that I have been granted indefinite leave to remain in this UK with my all my children and my granddaughter.

I couldn't believe it, I thought I was dreaming but it was really. I then started looking into the passports one by one and found that all the passports were stamped with an indefinite leave to remain visas. I shouted to myself, we have been granted Indefinite stay; and started to sing and dancing alone with tears of joy running on my cheeks. I put back the passports and the letter in the envelope and placed it on top of table.

Where There Is No Freedom or Peace There Is No Life

My sons had left home around 9.30am to town, after all these sadness of being in UK for all those years illegal. I picked my phone and called the Tony the elder son. Fortunately, he answered because most of the times he used not to answer his phone. and he used to return the calls when he sees the missed calls. When he answered his phone I asked him to come back home immediately with his brother Toddy.

Tony and Toddy were home in fifteen minutes, Tony opened the door as he used to have his keys. Both entered the house and saw me sitting on the sofa.

Mum are you alright? Tony asked

Yes, I'm very ok with a smile on my face. I answered

Why did you ask us to come home immediately, we were busy doing our things? Tody asked anxiously

Can you both sit down? I asked politely.

They both sat next to me on the sofa. I then picked the envelope from the table, hand it over the envelope to Tony to and asked him to open it.

Mum, this envelope is addressed to you; Tony said politely

While, Tony was talking to me Toddy the younger one grabbed the envelope and opened.

The envelope was not sealed so he opened it quickly and saw the passports and a letter.

These are passports mum, are we going back to Zimbabwe? Tody asked unhappy'

He then handover the passport and a letter to his big brother Tony.

Tony looked at me, and I asked him to open the letter, and read. He started reading while the younger brother Tody was busy looking at the passports one by one and found out all passports were stamped with indefinite leave to remain without restrictions in UK.

They both screamed with joy running around the house, singing, dancing it was our happiest day. Tony and Tody later came and knelt on the carpet in front of me and said mum thank you so much for being strong.

Mum I am now going to University, work some part time jobs and buy what we want. Tony explained happily. That evening I bought pizza for my children with the few pounds I had, just to celebrate our visas, my daughter joined us from her flat and we celebrated well. I slept well that night without worrying about visas or anything.

The next morning, I woke up around eight thirty, got out of bed and took all the bed linen in the washing machine. I took a shower, brushed my teeth and dressed in clean clothes. I headed downstairs to make some breakfast. Tony, Toddy and Lisa joined me in the kitchen and we all had breakfast together. My boys had bread with butter and jam, I had porridge and a cup of black coffee. My daughter had a cup of white tea and a plain slice of bread.

We were very happy that morning talking about our indefinite stay in UK without restrictions. Where there is no happiness, peace and freedom there is no peace.

After breakfast Tony rushed to the post office and sent his passport with a special delivery. Tody helped me to clean the house, washed the dishes. After some hours we decided to go out for walk and it started raining, while we still in the house and decided to stay indoors. It was a relaxing day for both of us, mental and physical and we were very happy.

Being granted an indefinite stay was a big thing in our lives as we had gained freedom to access all the things which were restricted and limited to us. The best thing we wanted to find jobs so that we can help ourselves not to continue depending on the money we were receiving from the government.

During this time of celebrating our freedom in this country, I started reflecting all what happened in Zimbabwe. I tried my best to put them behind and be happy but I had many issues inside me which I never spoke to anyone and kept haunting me. My childhood abuse was part of my life history, but never mentioned to anyone about all what I had experienced during war. This was very painful and sorrow and I was suffering inside.

When I tried to speak to my mother after I was released from hospital, she asked me to keep quite as it was a taboo in the community. I also tried to confide to Peter before marriage but he said he didn't want to know about it so I was bottling everything inside me.

At the age of fifteen was short and stayed in hospital, out of school, had no sense of achievement. From fifteen to eighteen years was the stage which I needed to develop my own sense of identity but unfortunately I had no sense of self, and also had lack sense of social roles, this made me to became confused. I had memory loss resulting me in isolation and withdrawn. I was haunted every day and night by the trauma of unspoken pain.

I tried my best to feel happy, but all of the sudden I could see myself as a failure, unlovable, worthless and became moody. I decided not to talk to anyone about the trauma because I assumed that I was not going to be listened.

This became worse and worse and my son Tody started to notice that something was bothering me but I was trying to make myself happy. He got very worried and when Tony came from University, they suggested that I should see the doctor.

My sons were now grown up to make decisions they couldn't understand what was happening to me and what was making me moody most of the times.

Meeting new people became a big challenge for me to an extent I could not make friends.

This went on for some months and after my children continued talking to me about going to the doctors and being checked. I later visited the doctor and prescribed depressive tablets,

I started taking them and they were making me sleepy a lot, but by the time I woke up; I reflected everything and this made me more terrified. I continued visiting doctors several times for check-ups, and all the time I got in the consultation room with the doctor or a nurse I could start sobbing silently without saying anything.

The doctor noticed and assumed that something was going on in my life.

'Eva' you always look sad and depressed all the time, you visited the doctors.

Is there anything worrying you? Doctor asked.

Nothing is worrying me, but I feel angry all the time; I replied

Would you like to speak with someone, about what makes you angry all the time, Doctor asked?

Who is that person you want me to speak with? I asked

The person is professional, and is called a counsellor, and you can talk to her, express all your feelings of what is bothering you and she will listen to you without judging you: doctor explained cheerfully

I did understand what the doctor had told me, and I asked him to make an appointment with the counsellor.

After a week, I received a call from unknown number. I answered it and asked who was calling.

The call was from the counsellor informing me that the appointment has been made for me to see the counsellor on such date.

My challenge was trusting people and I didn't know if I was going to trust the counsellor. I asked myself many questions, such as will the counsellor not think I am crazy?

Do I have to tell this counsellor everything about my past?

Do I just talk or discuss about my childhood and how will I feel after?

Is the counsellor being able to help me to come over what is distorting my life and what advice will I get from her.

I was asking myself all these questions and didn't get an answer. I didn't have any confidence and my esteem was very low.

I finally made up my mind and met the counsellor, it was difficult to express my feelings because of language barrier and what I needed most was to be listened not to be judged. The journey of processing my issues was not easy but I faced all the challenges and started to spit out things which I was bottling inside me.

The more I was talking about it, and being listened made me to feel better time to time. I started feeling sense of achievement and noticed that I have gained knowledge of many skills not by going to school but general life experience.

I then realised that in order for me to change my behaviour of mooting, I had to look things positive. This made it easy for me to be assertive personally and proved that I was as other person.

After having counselling sessions, I acquired decisions making, relationships forming strategies because relationship forming was one of my weakness that I had to deal with.

Being accountable of my decisions gave me sense of maturity and independence. I have also learned that sharing experiences gave me the confident I needed.

After a year 1n 2010 I was beginning to be impressed with the progress I have made. I started having a lot of interest in studying counselling.

I decided to go back to school and further my education to practice counselling, my aim was giving back to the society by helping other people who were suffering silently without knowing that they can speak up and been heard without being judged.

I wanted to help people to build their confidence, and also boost their esteem. As a woman of colour I acknowledged that at times I felt different from other people due to my skin, physical, appearance and difficulty in expressing myself in English as compared to the majority.

To help people who have been abused that, there are worth, valued and they should not look down on themselves thinking they are worthless. I was one of those people who suffered silently, tortured myself with questions, couldn't move on with life because of my past experience, and thought I was worthless

In the same year, I found a place at community College with the help of my son, as I was finding very difficult because of language barrier.

I started my education the following year 2011 in September by learning writing, speaking, listening, and reading. I started from entry three to level two which was equivalent to GSEC level. It was not an easy journey for me as I had dropped school at the age of fourteen years old. My challenge was to meet other classmates, coping with school work and meeting with different teachers was a struggle. It was very difficult to understand what I was taught by teachers because of language barrier.

I worked hard with the help of other students and teachers were fantastic. I passed my subjects and decide to study at higher education. I got a place at Havering College and was called for an interview for access to counselling and I passed the interview and was offered a place. This was the beginning of a journey of becoming a counsellor.

I didn't doubt this time but trusted in myself, and I wanted to take risk in my life and become a counsellor. I promised myself to work hard in this course and pass.

It all went well in the first year, because I had a lot of support from other students and tutors. In the process of becoming a counsellor I found that counsellors play a major role into people's lives. I have acquired a lot of knowledge and developed confidence which helped me dealing with issues of race, which I have been experiencing when I arrived in UK.

In my class I was the only black and old than other students. As a woman of colour I acknowledge that at times I felt different from other students due to my skin, physical, appearance and difficulty in expressing my feeling towards the subject.

I have come to realise how socially isolated I was. This caused a lot of anxiety, stress and a feeling powerless, but I have learnt that the more I understand myself is the wiser I became and wiser in understanding my feelings, meaning I become emotionally intelligent.

During my journey of becoming a counsellor, I also learnt that learning can be defined formally as an act, process or experience of gaining skills not only from classrooms but general life experiences. I am proudly to say I have gained diverse skills and I have obtained a lot of demonstrate, and I have started to feel confident, comfort and competent to meet other people and tell my story without fearing that people will judge me.

All the experiences and challenges have made me strong and realised that I have spent so many years of my life sad instead of living. Realising all the hurt and the pain from my childhood was a terrifying feeling but realised that what has happened has happened, and need to put behind the past, move on with my life. I have taught myself that I should not stress myself over the things I could not change.

I needed to bring myself back to the world and began to challenge all my fears, also believe in myself, no matter what other people think of me. I started building up myself, instead of tearing myself down by thinking of my past and my identity.

One of the hardest thing in my life was letting go, but when I had to tell my story, and it didn't make me cry, I was happy that I have overcame the challenges.

I finished my counselling in 2014 to a diploma level, and my children both graduated, working. Tony bought his house, he is very happy of what he acquired in life. Toddy working and living with his girlfriend very happy in their relationship.

I did work with young offenders after finishing my course and achieved what I wanted. I help more women to express their feelings. I have learnt how to communicate with others, I also learnt to listen and phrase to show that I'm listening. I have learned not judge or make assumptions. I am the happiest woman now with my children.